Ghosts of Princeton Battlefield

Ghosts of Princeton Battlefield

A walking tour play
of Princeton Battlefield State Park
Illustrating the history of the event
The Battle of Princeton
January 3, 1777

By Laura Crockett

Published by A Woman with a Past Productions
www.lauracrockett.com
Lauraspeaks@mac.com

Permission to perform this work must be obtained from the
author.

ISBN 978-0-97857139-9

CONTENTS

Forward

There are two version of *Ghosts Of Princeton Battlefield* included in this book; the *Ghost Hunter* version and the *Annis Boudinot Stockton* version. Both plays are site specific plays written for the purpose of edifying children of all ages about the awesome Battle of Princeton. They both follow the same general outline though there are some significant differences. The Ghost Hunter version focuses on entertaining children of all ages while it edifies them about the awesome Battle of Princeton that took place on January 3, 1777. The Mrs. Stockton character provides for a little more historical background on the Princeton/Stony Brook locale plus general American Revolutionary history as her husband, Richard Stockton, was a signer of the *Declaration of Independence* as was a prisoner of war for a few weeks during the winter of 1776-1777. There is also a Richard Stockton version but I have decided not to include here.

The inspiration for this particular type of entertainment came from the smash hit play, Tamara, which ran for 11 years in Los Angeles. The audience for Tamara did not sit in chairs in front of a stage. Instead, they wandered from room to room of the "palace" following the action as they followed the various characters. The second inspiration came from a walk-through theatre event staged in New Jersey. This concept was brought to my attention my Princeton Battlefield Trustee, Robert Rosetta.

Ghosts of Princeton Battlefield, Ghost Hunter version, was produced on Princeton Battlefield during the summer of 2008. It was directed by Joe Doyle of Actor's Net of Buck's County. It was produced by Cheryl Doyle, Kip Cherry and Ruth Ann Mitchell. Members of the Actor's Net Theater took on the many roles bringing the words on the pages to life. I am forever grateful to that team for their skill and boldness in taking on this project.

I am also in debt to Princeton Battlefield State Park's Site History Specialist, John Mills. His patience in answering all of my questions and guiding my research is truly valued. Writers of historical material cannot advance their projects without such assistance.

Finally, the love I have for the wondrous history of our unique nation cannot be overstated. If you were to accuse me of placing the United States on a pedestal I would agree with you. We were founded by a set of men that the world sees only too rarely. My attempt is to illuminate this tiny bit of our founding and founders it in order to preserve our tangible history along side the collective knowledge of the events. Princeton Battlefield is a magical place. It is beautiful and haunted. And it needs your help. Please listen to the characters in this play as they tell you how you can be a part of history by preserving the past for the future.

Yours in liberty,
Laura Crockett

Ghost Hunter Version

Note: Except for the *Ghost Hunter*, all the characters are ghosts. They are benign ghosts. Their purpose is to tell a story and the only haunting they do is to urge people to support and care for Princeton Battlefield State Park and its museum, the Clarke House.

The ghosts have ashen skin and blue lips. The clothing they wear shows the wear and dust of the grave. Many of the soldiers have dirt on their decaying uniforms as they were not buried in coffins but thrown into mass graves. Some of the soldiers may also have dried up blood or other indications of wounds on their bodies.

The *Ghost Hunter* is dressed in modern day clothing. He has been investigating sightings of paranormal activity on Princeton Battlefield State Park. He carries a device for finding ghostly activity.

Casting the play

Experienced actors of any level, professional or amateur, may be used. Re-enactors can be brought in to play the soldiers. It is okay for the soldiers to make up throwaway lines as they are running around playing at war.

The performances can be recycled (a new group) every 20 minutes if you have 2 actors to play the following characters: The Ghost Hunter, Mercer, Sally. All together there are 10 speaking parts, requiring about 14 - 16 performers or 17 - 19 if you wish to recycle the play every 20 minutes. If you do not use the recycle protocol, after every two performances, the actors should have a 15-minute break.

Historical Characters

Hugh Mercer, 52,

Captain William Shippin, 26, a Marine

Thomas Clarke, 35

Hannah Clarke, his sister, 28

Fictional characters

The Ghost Hunter

Jimmy, a 14 year-old Continental Army Drummer Boy

Mary, a 12 year-old girl living in Stony Brook

Sally, a serving girl of 16, lives with Mary's family

Ezra, fortyish, A Pennsylvania Militiaman

Peter, an American Marine, 18, (black)

Harry, thirtyish, a British Regular

Plus various Continental and Regular soldiers

SETTING UP THE ACTION

Ghosts of Princeton Battlefield is a site-specific play. All action takes place on Princeton Battlefield State Park. It is written so that the audience, or *Tourists*, move from scene to scene and, at times, follow the Ghosts to the next scene. The action throughout the performance must be kept dynamic. The actors need to be comfortable with the audience "in their face" as well as be aware where the audience is so that they do not bump into them. At times, the Ghosts address the audience directly. These sections are written as appeals to the audience to become involved in the issues surrounding the battlefield. They are meant to reach the heart as well as the mind. An actor that is a patriot and a preservationist will be best at conveying the urgency of the issues.

The action needs to begin close to the Clarke House. If permission is granted, the porch room and steps may be used in the first scene. The use of the Clarke House, either of its interior or exterior, *should not be attempted without the express permission of the site history specialist.*

The action of the play takes place within a semi-circular area, beginning with the north side of the CH and ending at the smokehouse on the south side of the CH. The action starts on the north side porch, continues on at the orchard east of the house, moves east again to the trail (Eastern trail) that leads through a wooded area, then to the open field. It then moves south across the open field to a second trail that leads west (Western trail) through the wooded area. The final scene is played out at the end of this trail near the smokehouse.

The play opens on the porch located on the north side of the CH (Ghost Hunter/Mary/Sally.) The characters/Tourists then move east to the next scene in the orchard (Ezra/Jimmy/Mary/Sally/Mercer/GH.) From this orchard they take the eastern trail into the wooded area. Beginning battle scenes take place here (Harry/Mercer/Continentals/Regulars.) Again the Tourists follow the action east to the open field. The Mercer ambush takes place here, (Mercer/Harry/Continentals/Regulars) as well as the Mary/Sally/Shippin/Peter scene.

Once the girls are rescued, the Tourists and GH head west along the Western Trail. The next scene is the Shippin/Peter scene, after which the Tourists again walk west to nearly the end and the Mercer/Thomas/Hannah/Sally scene. The play ends with the Tourists following the GH back up to the CH.

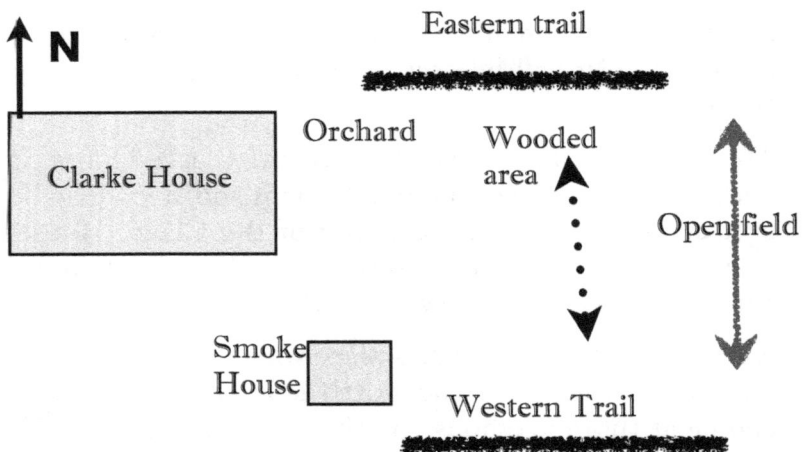

Map not to scale

The wooded areas can be used by the cast as entrance and exit points along the trails, the trees may be used as stand ins for buildings or places for soldiers to hide behind.

There are other alternatives to this basic setup, including special use of the CH if permitted, for Mercer's final death scene.

The best time of year to produce the play is in the fall when the vegetation has thinned somewhat. The action can take place during the day or night if sufficient lighting is available. The actual historical action took place during the daylight hours, so it is recommended that this be performed during the same.

Scene 1

*The tour begins as soon as a group of Tourists are gathered.
From a strategic spot, the Ghost Hunter enters at a run,
yelling at the Tourists. He is dressed casually. Across his
head are earplugs that are connected to a device that he uses
to listen for ghosts.*

Ghost Hunter: They're empty! The graves! They're
empty! (Calming) I gota catch my breath. This is
somethin' really somethin'. Oh, let me tell you who I
am. I'm a ghost hunter. I was called out here by the
state of New Jersey because there have been some
odd things happening here on Princeton Battlefield.
Ya know, plasmatic activity. Things that go bump in
the night. Right here, on these grounds and in that
house. (*Points to Clarke House*) Rumor has it, or at
least it's what I've been hearing, that the place is
being haunted because the dead are angry. Yes.
They're not happy about certain developments. But
hey, I don't get involved in all that. I just do my job,
look for ghosts.   I went up there (indicates the
Columns) to check out the graves. Yeah, soldiers are
buried up there. Did you know that? Well I'm not
mincin' my words. Lots of plasmatic activity up there.
I'm tellin' ya, ya gotta be careful around here because
I saw a big hold in the ground where one wasn't
before.

SOUND of marching is heard.

7

GH: Somethin's goin' on-Wait, what's that? (*To Tourists*) Do you hear it too? Yeah, marchin'.

The GH places his earplugs into his ears, and listens to his "plasmatic device." A look of grateful surprise crosses his face. Just as this happens, the ghost of Mary walks out of the CH. She is dressed in simple Quaker clothing, but in her Sunday best. It is her grave dress: Dusty, moldy, perhaps with a few bugs on it along with a bit of her flesh eaten away. Mary concentrates on the road before her, her eyes follow the marching. Mary ignores the GH. The GH places his device near her.

GH: Oh. (*Testing Mary.*) She's dead.

Mary: (*In a loud whisper*) What is this?

Sally: (*Voice only*) Mary? Mary, where are you?

Mary: (*Loud whisper*) Out here, Sally.

Sally's face can be seen peering out the window. She expresses shock to see Mary standing on the porch. Sally walks out of the house. As Mary and Sally dialogue, the GH tests Sally as well.

Sally: What are you doing out here? It's barely sunrise.

Mary: Look at all the soldiers. Where are they going?

8

Sally: (*Turning her attention to the road*) I don't know.

GH: She is very dead. Wow, this is somethin', two ghosts materializing in one day!

Sally: Tis terribly cold. Where is your cloak?

Mary: Tis January, Sally. I expect it to be cold.

Sally: January Third to be exact.

GH: Wait, wait, that date, (*rummages through his pockets for a piece of paper*) it means something out here. (*Find paper, reads*) Yeah, here it is. Say that's the date of the big battle out here.

Sally: You had best come in and dress.

Mary: Not yet. I have to know where they are going. (*Mary steps off the steps as if to follow the troops.*)

Sally: (*Looking closely out at the road.*) These are Continentals. Look! Isn't that General Washington?

Mary: Thee knows what he looks like?

Sally: Aye. He was pointed out to me when he came through here before, in December. He looked weary then. Not so now.

Mary: And now he is here, in Stony Brook. (*With dismay.*) Do you think he lost that battle yesterday?

Sally: You mean the guns we heard coming from Trenton?

Mary: Uh-huh.

Sally: It must have been a fierce battle, such a noise it was. It seemed to go on for hours.

Mary: Dost think they will have a battle here?

Sally: Lord, I pray to God no.

Mary: I think I see someone I know.

Sally: Among the soldiers?

Mary: Yes.

Sally: Well, you will have to save your re-acquaintance for some other time, miss, and come in now to dress.

Mary: Oh Sally, thee forgets, we have no clothes.

Sally: What do you mean, what is this we're wearing?

Mary: Our burial clothes. Remember, we are dead.

Sally: Such foolishness, girl.

Mary: What thee forgets, every year, and every year what I tell thee again, is that we are as dead as door nails And every year I have to hold up the mirror so that thee can see what is the truth. Thee is dead. (*To GH*) And thee may put thy device away.

GH: Oh. Oh! Do you always speak to humans?

Mary: (*Continues to GH*) When the need is there.

GH: And right now?

Mary: Sally and I are like ghosts everywhere that haunt certain places. When there is a need to tell our story, the story of this place, (*Indicates park*) then we materialize. This we must do because folks have a way of forgetting. (*Focuses back onto the road in front.*) Look! Is it who I think it is? (*Straining to see*) Yes! It's Jimmy Updyke!

Sally: Shshsh, Mary. Not too loud. Now come back in. Those soldiers want quiet.

Mary: Oh, I would follow them…

Sally: (*Grabbing hold of Mary*) No, young lady. You are to come inside. Now!

Mary: (*Twisting free*) No Sally, today I will live again!

Mary runs toward the orchard as Jimmy and Ezra come around the corner. Mary runs toward him, Sally following, the GH and the Tourists following the girls. As soon as Jimmy spots Mary he smiles as he places his finger on his lips to tell her to keep quiet. As the GH runs ahead he keeps his device trained on the ghosts ahead of him. He tests Jimmy and then Ezra.

GH: Dead. (*Swallow hard*) Ghosts soldiers on a battlefield. Not a good sign.

Mary: Jimmy, I did not know if ever I would see thee again.

Jimmy: Mary, Sally, you best go back to your house.

Mary: But we have to know, what happened in Trenton?

Ezra: We must be to Prince Town?

Jimmy: Not quite, Ezra. We are in Stony Brook. This is my friend, Mary and her serving girl, Sally.

Ezra: Well youngin's, I think we have a little time. Talk with us a spell.

Sally: What happened yesterday? We heard such an awful noise coming from Trent Town.

Jimmy: You heard about us taking the Hessians in Trenton in December?

Sally: Aye.

Jimmy: Yesterday, we returned. And, (*turns to Ezra*) Well, I think you have to begin, Ezra, tell them about you and Colonel Hand.

Ezra: It was like this. When General Howe, in New York, heard what we had done, takin' back Trenton the way we did, he sent General Cornwallis in to be rid of us once and for all. General Washington knew they would come for us, to Trenton. So he waited. But first he sent Colonel Hand out with six hundred of us Pennsylvania riflemen. Our duty was clear. We had to keep the British Regular troops out of Trenton for as long as we could. So we met up with 'em over yonder, in Maidenhead. From behind trees and barns or anything we could find to hide behind, we took shots at Cornwallis' soldiers. Then we would disappear into the woods and wait for 'em to advance a little more. But once we had pinned 'em down two or three times, they got to feelin' skittish about this entire business of marching into Trenton So they slowed down and took their time. But God's weather helped us as well, for it was warm enough to melt the icy roads.

Mary: Stuck were they?

Ezra: And the Hessians cursin' to get at us. But held they were until nearly dark when we reached Trenton.

Jimmy: Those of us in Trenton were preparing. I was with my fellows in the fife and drum when General Washington had us all pull back, across the bridge, you remember, by the mill. There is only one bridge across the Assunpink. The river is deep there, near where it empties out into the Delaware. The water was angry because so much snow had melted. I confess, I was scared due to the talk among our men; that the Hessians coming with Cornwallis were out for revenge. We could hear the exchanges between Colonel Hand's men and the British coming closer and closer. Then we saw them, Hands men firing down the streets of Trenton, and we knew it wouldn't be long before the British got to us. (*Pauses*)

Mary: What happened then, Jimmy?

Jimmy: I will tell you Mary, because I will never forget it for as long as I live.

Mary: Tell, Jimmy, tell.

Jimmy: As we were crossing over the Assunpink, General Washington was sitting on his horse in the middle of the bridge. Hundreds of us were making our way, so it was crowded. As I made my way across I got shoved a bit to the side, against the horse. That horse was so calm, not a flinch he gave. And

Washington no different in that he was composed and watching over us. And then he looked down on me, me, and said, "Keep safe son." I shall never forget that, Mary. Never.

Mary: No, Jimmy, thee will never forget that.

Sally: But how are ye here?

Ezra: Well, youngin' though Cornwallis invited us, we decided not to accept his invitation to dance in Trenton. We pulled out at midnight last night. We left fires burnin' bright, so as to fool 'em. Why those Regulars are, most likely, still asleep thinkin' we are waiting for them to attack us. But we marched this way instead, to take Nassau Hall and the stores inside, for ourselves.

Mary: That's why thee has marched this way!

Ezra: Here comes General Mercer.

Enter Mercer and his men. Seeing him, Sally is struck with a young girl's infatuation for the neatly attired Brig. General Mercer.

Jimmy: I have to leave now, Mary. Go back. Now. (*Mary and Sally begin to walk back towards the house.*)

Ezra: (*Reacting to something he has seen*) What was that?

Exit Ezra and Jimmy, enter Harry and a British soldier from across the way. Mary and Sally hide behind a tree. During the following dialogue, soldiers should be running round, always headed in the same direction, toward the open space at the end of the trail.

Harry: What is that you saw? (*Looking out into the "distance"*) Yes, I see them. The Americans. Here!

Mercer: Captain Neill!

Harry: Come about! Double quick! We'll hide here behind the barn.

Mercer: Follow me!

Harry: Stay hidden behind the barn!

Wait briefly, if needed, for the tourists to catch up to the action in the open field.

Harry: Hold your fire!

The Americans do not see the Brits hiding in wait for them.

Mercer: Into the orchard!

Mercer runs forward and the Brits fire.

Harry: Fire!

Mercer: Captain Neil, give me artillery fire!

Harry: Make haste lads, their cannon are positioned!

SOUND of cannon fire, followed by musket fire. The girls scream. The GH hits the ground.

GH: These are ghosts! They are not supposed to have firing weapons!

Harry: Engage the ragged rebels! (*Runs out into the open field*)

With the SOUND of gunfire in the BG, the soldiers break into hand-to-hand combat. The one American soldier is killed. Mercer is hit in the head. He goes down on his knees. He draws his sword to fit off the two Brits. They over power him and he is knocked in the head a second time.

Harry: Ask for quarter you damn rebel general!

Harry and Mercer fight a bit more, and then Mercer is bayoneted by both soldiers. He falls as if dead. Sally screams and clutches Mary.

Sally: They've killed him!

Mary: Shush, Sally, shush.

The Brits move off. The SOUND of battle continues. Enter Captain Shippin and Peter.

Peter: (*Spotting the girls*) Captain Shippin!

Shippin: (*To the girls*) You should not be here.

Mary: We-

Shippin: Peter, we need to get them to safety.

Peter: (*To the girls, pointing opposite*) Whose barn is that?

Mary: Thomas Clarke's barn.

Peter: That will have to do. Come along.

Shippin: See that their safe, Peter, then catch us further on! (*Exits)*

Peter: Aye sir!

Mary: Who are thee?

Peter: Captain Shippin and I are Continental Marines.

Peter hustles the girls off the playing area and into the woods. The GH motions for the Tourists to follow him as he walks down the south/west trail.

Ghost Hunter: Let's see if I can't get you outa here because this is intense. This way.

Scene 2

As the Tourists walk Peter runs out of the woods, and very near the Tourists. A large volley is heard. Peter stops still.

Peter: Captain! Captain Shippin!

Shippin comes out of the woods, clutching his gut. The Tourists may gather in closely.

Shippin: Peter? Is it over?

Peter: Washington is pursuing the Regulars.

Shippin: He is alive?

Peter: Yes, he is.

Shippin: I was stunned after I was hit. Tell me, what happened?

Peter: After Mercer went down the men routed.

Shippin: Mercer is dead?

Peter: Honestly sir, I don't know. Most likely. He was bayoneted, repeatedly.

Shippin: He is a good man. But continue, Peter, what happened then?

Peter: As the men were running back, away from the fight, General Washington charged out onto the field, telling them to regroup. "Go back, go back!" He shouted. But they were frightened, overwhelmed. Washington rode his horse round the men, shouting out words of encouragement. "There are more of us than them!" he shouted out. And then "Go back, go back and let us claim our victory!" He turned his steed round again, and road, straightforward, into the battle.

Shippin: Into the battle? Into the flanks, you mean? To urge the men on from the sides?

Peter: No, Captain. I mean into the middle of it. *Into the middle*, sir. When he got to the center of the field his horse reared up and then men gave a shout. Do you recall it sir? The British lined up in battle formation right in front of him.

Shippin: (*Pauses to think*) Yes! I do recall it....

Peter: Because you were there, sir, in the midst yourself.

Shippin: I was in the frontal attack. I had just fired my weapon when I heard a great shout coming from behind me. I stepped to the side, to reload and to try and see what had happened among the men.

Peter: It was him; Washington, racing onto the field.

Shippin: Yes. I was afraid for him, that he would be killed.

Peter: Without turning your back to the enemy, you ran, backwards, then fired your weapon upon some poor fool who lies over yonder, drenched in his own blood. He won't be going home.

Shippin: I knelt down, not too far from him, I reloaded again.

Peter: Washington rode to the center, in between the enemy and us.

Shippin: He is our ideal, of what should be done. I remember standing, thinking to shield him...

Peter. So you did.

Shippin: And I can remember nothing else save an awful roar of fire.

Peter: Both sides fired, at the same time. Guns, cannon, all conspired to bring him, and all men, down. The last thing I saw was you, Captain. You leapt up as if to catch something. Then a great smoke filled the air, like a thick fog. There was no breeze to vanquish that smoke, so, for what seemed an eternity, we could see nothing. We were petrified, that when the smoke cleared, we should be without our commander.

Shippin: And?

Peter: The smoke lifted enough so that we could see him, the general, still sitting upon his horse.

Shippin: Wounded?

Peter: No.

Shippin: Not anything?

Peter: Not a scratch.

Shippin: I am pleased to hear it.

Peter: We all were pleased. (*Turns to face Shippin*) But you, Captain, you, I am afraid, did not fare as well.

Shippin: What does that matter?

Peter: It matters to me. William Shippin, you have been like an older brother to me. You have kept me alive.

Shippin: We have kept each other afloat during these past few months.

Peter: I have not been much help to you in this battle at Princeton.

Shippin: You are here with me now. Your arm, Peter, it does not look to be of much use to you.

Peter: (*Feeling for arm*) Cannon.

Shippin: Does it cause you much pain?

Peter: I feel nothing.

Shippin: Neither do I. (*Looks at wound*) It is clean through my gut, Peter.

Peter: Yes, I know.

Shippin: Why don't I feel it?

Peter: You don't remember?

Shippin: Remember what?

Peter: Captain, when they fired upon our general, you jumped up to shield his body.

Shippin: (*Slowly remembering*) I begin to have a sense of what has really happened to me.

Peter: Do you sir?

Shippin: Peter, am I…

Peter: (*Quickly, to the point*) Yes, you are dead, sir.

Shippin: And you?

Peter: Dead as dead can be.

Shippin: How are we to fight for our country this way?

Peter: I'm not certain. Though I think I have an idea.

Shippin: What's that?

Peter: Something has happened here, on this field, to bring us back. Something unusual for out of the corner of my eye I've noticed strange things.

Shippin: (*Focusing on the tourists.*) You mean like them? (*Points to them*)

At this point, Peter notices the GH testing him with his device. Peter points his weapon at the GH.

GH: (Putting up hands) I don't mean any harm.

Shippin: Who are you? Who are they?

GH: We're just Americans.

Shippin: What do you mean, "just Americans?"

GH: You know. Citizens of the country you died to build?

Shippin: Citizens? You mean we won? (*GH nods head*) Peter, we won. There's a United States of America. (*To GH*) But why are we here now? Can you tell me that?

GH: Not too many American remember you?

Shippin: How do you care for that news, Peter. We spill our blood upon this field and this is our thanks for it? Forgotten, as if it never happened?

GH: It's been a long time.

Shippin: I did not step into this battle for any fame or glory. Yet here's the thing; I would do it all over again. Would it be too much to ask of you to remember me? And this young lad here, only 18 when he paid the price?

GH: Every Marine who fought on this field is remembered, Captain. Inside the Clarke House. You're listed. Peter is remembered too. But not too many people enter that old house. I think that's why you're here today, haunting the place. To remind us about not just what happened here, but who was involved.

Shippin: Then remember us and tell your friends about what you have seen here.

Shippin and Peter back up into the woods and are swallowed up by the trees and shadows. Shippin's and Peter's voice can be heard saying; "Remember us."

The GH now leads the group to the next scene, Mercer dying in the Clarke House. Mercer lies in the bed, Sally there to comfort him. She cleans his wounds, straightens his blankets and so forth.

Mercer: Is it over?

Sally: Aye. Tis over.

Mercer: And?

Sally: You're alive.

Mercer: (*With slight exasperation*) The battle. What was the outcome?

Thomas: The Americans took the day.

Mercer: We won. And Washington, the army?

Hannah: Gone on to Morristown.

Thomas: Washington made haste after the battle as Cornwallis was at the bridge point and pressing his men across the brook.

Mercer: Aside from yourselves, who attends me?

Hannah: Dr. Rush. Poor man, he needs sleep. Day and night he makes his rounds, first here then the Meeting House where more poor souls lay sick, wounded or dying. He has also looked in on my poor sister-in-law, who lost her child from the womb the day before the battle.

Mercer: A miscarriage?

Hannah: Yes.

Mercer: We were not the cause of it you say?

Hannah: No. Though who can say with all this stimulation these past weeks... They hid her in the cellar as the shooting started. Carried her down, bed and all. The Regulars were not kind to her once the Continentals had left. Most distressing it has been these past weeks.

Thomas: Lesser men it was who thought to question her in a rough manner, but then Cornwallis put a stop to it.

Mercer: I am sorry for the trouble it has caused you for I see you have worked tirelessly to care for *all* men wounded in this battle.

Hannah: It makes little difference to a man, as he lay dying, whether he is Rebel or Regular. I doubt if God recognizes such differences.

Mercer: Aye good mistress Clarke. That must be the way of it where men have no say. All the same, as I lay dying I thank you, and your brother, for your kindness.

Sally: Surely general, you will recover.

Mercer: I think not lass.

Thomas: Thee would have fared better if the British would had given thee the asked for quarter.

Mercer: No, that is not the way of it, and I must tell you how it was before I die.

Hannah: You'll not die this day, General Mercer.

Mercer: I will die soon.

Sally: (*pointing out wounds on chest*) These wounds seem to heal.

Mercer: This is what shall kill me. (*He raises his arm*)

Sally: (*Gasps*) But Dr. Rush-

Mercer: ...has done what he can. Attend my words. When I received the second blow to the head, the Regulars bade me give up. They called me Rebel. Me. Hugh Mercer. They cannot know how I think of *them* as rebels, who overthrew the rightful king of England, for that German.

Sally: You are speaking of the troubles of 1746, and of Bonny Prince Charlie.

Mercer: I am.

Hannah: In Scotland. What was that place?

Mercer: Culloden.

Sally: I heard my father tell of it. A terrible day it was, for the Scots who sided with Charles Stewart. Were you hunted down, Hugh Mercer?

Mercer: I was. Like we were rabid dogs, killing or taking us prisoners to be sold into slavery. I hid myself for a year before I had money enough to come to America. But once here, all that terror was forgotten.

Hannah: Until the Third of January?

Mercer: Aye, Mistress Clarke, until then, (*becoming agitated*) when they spoke to me as they did and I in my own land, not theirs!

Sally: You must lye still, General Mercer.

Mercer: I don't mean to be trouble, lass.

Sally: You're none at all, if you stay quiet and don't rile yourself so.

Hannah: The battle is over, and for myself, I am relieved. Tis not any thing I would ever wish to live through again.

Mercer: I am sorry for it having to be here, on this farm. And you being Friends…

Thomas: Twas William's farm that felt the brunt of it.

Mercer: His orchard, was it, where I took the blows?

Thomas: Thee wast telling us of the stabbing thee took.

Mercer: Aye. I will set the record aright. I would not give them the pleasure of my asking for their mercy. I sought no quarter from them and accept my punishment accordingly. That I angered them, and these wounds are their response, tis only what was expected.

Thomas: I understand.

Mercer: *(sighs deeply)* What day is it?

Thomas: First Day.

Mercer: How many days since the battle?

Thomas: Nine.

Hannah: Tis the 12th day of January.

Mercer: I feel that they will now remember me.

Thomas: *(Leans in close to Mercer)* The Regulars remember thee. They come into the room at times to stare down at thee.

Hannah: Shshsh!

Mercer: No, not the Regulars. *(Turns his head towards the Tourists)* Them.

Thomas: Them?

Hannah: The guests out there. They've come to be haunted by us.

Thomas: What dost thee mean, "haunted by us?"

Hannah: Brother, you know you are dead.

Thomas: I'm no such thing. I am very old, and well preserved.

Hannah: I cannot say the same for our house. It has been too many years since we have been there to care for it. Ask them, (*Looks out to Tourists*) Thomas, to care for it.

Thomas: (*To Tourists*) My sister speaks the truth. We are only spirits here for the day. We need you to take care of our house for us because now it really belongs to all Americans. Will you do that for us?

Hannah: And what else? (*She steps back toward the trees.*)

Thomas: (*Referring to Mercer.*) You can see the room where this great man died. (*Refers to the Clarke House.*) Tis the bedroom in the back of the house. But presently our time here is growing short and as ghosts of Princeton Battlefield we cannot travel beyond the borders of this park. We depend on thee to bring the story to all. Tell everyone what you have heard here; that 233 years back brave Americans fought and died to start a unique nation. (*He turns to leave, and then remembers something, turns back.*) Make history for thyself by leaving something behind. Keep in mind that when ever thee touches the walls of the Clarke House, ten, twenty or a hundred years from this day someone else will touch that same place.

They will then touch thee, will they not? For this house stands because thou hast cared to make it so. (*Walks to trees, then turns back*) Remember us.

Thomas disappears into the background. The GH steps forward to distract the crowd.

GH: My readings are growing dim. The ghosts are going. Let's see if we find anymore this way. (*Leads them back towards the CH*) No, they're gone. But they'll be back again. You can count on it. Come back here to Princeton Battlefield whenever you can. And bring your friends. (*If the CH is open, suggest tour.*) Why don't we do as Thomas Clarke suggested and go into the Clarke House to see where they lived and where Mercer died.

End

Annis Boudinot Stockton Version

THE CHARACTERS

All the characters are ghosts. They are benign ghosts. Their purpose is to tell a story and the only haunting they do is to urge people to support and care for Princeton Battlefield State Park and its museum, the Clarke House.

The ghosts have ashen skin and blue lips. The clothing they wear shows the wear and dust of the grave. Many of the soldiers have dirt on their decaying uniforms as they were not buried in coffins but thrown into mass graves. Some of the soldiers may also have dried up blood or other indications of wounds on their bodies.

Mrs. Stockton is dressed in a plain dress of the era. Since she must at times walk rapidly, it is best to keep the actor in comfortable shoes. If the weather is chilly, a cloak may be worn.

Casting the play

As with the Ghost Hunter version, the best cast is to use those with a passion for the subject matter. Re-enactors can be employed throughout, especially as the soldiers. For this play there are 14 speaking parts. Annis and General Mercer are the characters that are best double cast if the play is to be recycled every 20 minutes.

The ages for the characters run from 12 year-old Mary to Mercer who is 52.

Historical Characters

Annis B. Stockton, 35

Brigadier General Hugh Mercer, 52

Captain William Shippin, 26, a Marine

Thomas Clarke, 35

Hannah Clarke, 28, his sister

Colonel Mawhood (British)

General Washington

Fictional

Jimmy, a 14-year-old Continental Army Drummer Boy

Mary, a 12 year-old girl living in Stony Brook

Sally, a serving girl of 16, lives with Mary's family

Martin, a Private in the Continental Army

Ezra, A Pennsylvania Militiaman

Peter, an American Marine, 18, (black)

Harry, a British Regular

SETTING UP THE ACTION

The set up for the action remains the same semi-circular route. Mrs. Stockton may approach the Tourists from inside the Clarke House, if permissible.

She may approach them by coming around the corner of the CH or if the group meets on the south side of the house, she may stand on the porch to speak to them before leading them to the north side of the house.

The action then continues on the porch located on the north side of the CH (Annis/Mary/Sally.) The characters/Tourists then move east to the next scene in the orchard (Ezra/Jimmy/Mary/Sally/Martin/Annis.) From this orchard they take the eastern trail into the wooded area. Beginning battle scenes take place here (Mawhood/Harry/Mercer/Continentals/Regulars.) Again the Tourists follow the action east to the open field. The Mercer ambush takes place here, (Mawhood/Mercer/Harry/Continentals/Regulars) as well as the Mary/Sally/Shippin/Peter scene.

Once the girls are rescued, the Tourists and Annis head west along the Western Trail. The next scene is the Shippin/Peter scene, after which the Tourists again walk west to nearly the end and the Mercer/Thomas/Hannah scene. The play ends with the Tourists following Annis toward the CH.

Scene 1

The tour begins when the ghost of Annis Boudinot Stockton approaches the gathered audience members arranged in groups of 20 or less. These groups will be referred to as Tourists.

Annis (*approaching the Tourists*): Welcome to Princeton Battlefield. I am Annis Boudinot Stockton. I live in Prince Town, in a house called Morven. I am a poetess and the wife of Richard Stockton, who is a signer of the Declaration of Independence. Unfortunately, Richard is dead. Come to think of it, so am I. What does that matter; I don't feel dead. Indeed, I feel quite alive. Let me ask you, (*pick out Tourist to speak to*) do you think I am a ghost? You say *I am* a ghost? Well, I don't know what to say. (*Looking a Tourist in the face.*) I don't frighten you do I? Oh, I am so relieved to hear that I do not haunt in an injurious manner.

I am here to tell you about events that took place on the Clarke Farms 233 years ago. The winter of 1776 was a terrible time for us. Our army lost New York to the British. They then chased Washington and his troops across New Jersey. It seemed to us that we had lost our glorious revolution. For me, personally it was a distressing time because Richard was taken prisoner by American loyalist. As he was considered a traitor he was treated harshly. But it didn't end there. When the British soldiers arrived in Prince Town they took over our home (*with emotion*) and then proceeded to destroy all of the beautiful books in our library.

After chasing the Americans across the Delaware into Pennsylvania General Cornwallis left soldiers here in New Jersey to keep the Americans pinned down. Cornwallis then returned to New York. That's when something wonderful happened. Washington and the American army crossed the Delaware and took Trenton back! We were overjoyed to hear the news! But then General Cornwallis retuned and marched his thousands of troops through Princeton. He left hundreds of soldiers in Nassau Hall. He then went on to Trenton. That day was January 2, 1777. (*Pause, listens*) Wait, what is that I hear?

The SOUND of soldiers marching is now heard in the BG. Annis leads the Tourists to the house steps.

The Clarke House is a stand in for a house in Stony Brook along the road the American army is taking toward Princeton. From out of the house steps the ghost of Mary. She is dressed in a simple skirt and top. She concentrates her eyes out onto the road, straining to see what she hears.

Mary: What is this?

Sally: (*Voice only*) Mary? Mary, where are you? (*Sally's face can be seen peering out the window. She expresses shock to see Mary standing on the porch.*)

38

Mary: (*Loud whisper*) Out here, Sally.

Sally walks out of the house.

Sally: What are you doing out here? It's barely sunrise.

Mary: Look at all the soldiers. Where are they going?

Sally: I don't know, but it's cold. Where is your cloak?

Mary: It is January, Sally. I expect it to be cold.

Sally: January Third to be exact. And you have chores to do.

Mary: Not yet. I have to know where they are going. (*Mary steps off the steps as if to follow the troops.*)

Sally: (*Looking closely out at the road.*) These are Continentals, not the British that came through here yesterday. Look! Isn't that General Washington?

Mary: Is it?

Sally: Yes.

Mary: And now he is here, in Stony Brook. (*With dismay.*) Do you think he lost that battle yesterday?

Sally: You mean the sound of the guns we heard coming from Trenton yesterday?

Mary: Uh-huh.

Sally: It must have been a fierce battle, such a noise it was for all those hours.

Mary: Do you think they will have a battle here?

Sally: Lord, I pray to God no.

Mary: I think I see someone I know.

Sally: Marching with this lot?

Mary: Yes.

Sally: Well, you will have to save your reacquaintance for some other time, miss, and come in now to dress.

Mary: Oh Sally, you forget, we have no clothes.

Sally: What do you mean, what is this we're wearing?

Mary: That what we were buried in. Remember? We are dead.

Sally: Such foolishness, girl.

Mary: You forget every year that we are as dead as door nails And every year I have to hold up the mirror so that you can see that you can't be seen.

Sally: I see you, and you are without a cloak.

Mary: But I can feel nothing. Seems I must remind thee again how we materialize we need to tell this story, and de-materialize when we are finished.

Sally: But it's January 3rd, 1777.

Mary: Sally, we are like ghosts everywhere who materialize.

As Sally steps forward to speak, the marching SOUND fades more into the BG.

Sally: Oh yes, yes, I know, but I don't want to frighten the children. (*to a child*) I haven't frightened you, have I? (*Depending on answer*)
  Response 1: Good. Because Mary and I have to begin a story…
  Response 2: I didn't mean to frighten you, but Mary and I have to begin a story…
(*Sally continues:*)) of why we come back here to this plot of Earth. You will see other ghosts, but no one will harm you. I am sorry to say that you will see some sad things as well as happy ones….

Mary: Look! (*The SOUND of marching gains in intensity*) Is that...? (*Straining to see*) Oh yes, it is. It's Jimmy Updyke!

The soldiers of the Continental Army now come into view down the lane. Annis points them out to the Tourists.

Sally: Shshsh, Mary. Not too loud. Now come back in. Those soldiers want quiet.

Mary: Oh, I would follow them...

Sally: (*Grabbing hold of Mary*) Nay, young lady. You are to come inside this minute.

Mary: Nothing of the sort Sally. Come with me instead and let us live again!

Mary pulls Sally along and they follow the soldiers.

Annis: Oh, girls, wait! (*To Tourists*) Come along then, the game is on! (*She leads them to Scene 2*)

Scene 2

In the orchard. Mary and Sally hide as they watch for soldiers.

Annis: What's that they see? Look, over there.

Annis points out an area. Out of the trees walk three ghosts, the first being Jimmy Updyke, drummer boy for the Continental Army. He walks with a muffled drum. The other two soldiers walk on either side of him. One is Martin, a continental and the other is Ezra, a militiaman.

Ezra: Youngin'. Are we there yet?

Jimmy: No sir, we're not. This is Stony Brook. It's another mile or so to the College of New Jersey. Straight ahead we shall soon see the Friends' Meetin' House and then the Clarke's.

Martin: Who are the Clarkes?

Jimmy: Thomas and William. Brothers with farms side by side, not too far from Nassau Hall itself.

Martin: This is rich land, lots of farms here.

Jimmy: Including my family's land, and the Stumps. These are their fields.

Mary: (*Whispers to Sally*) He mentions us.

Sally: Aye Mary Stump, so he does.

Ezra: Their stopping up ahead.

Martin: So they are.

Jimmy: It feels good to be so near home.

Martin: I have a feelin' too. It's called hunger.

Ezra: We all feel that.

Jimmy: I feel amazed. These past few weeks have been days I will never forget.

Martin: None of us will forget Trenton.

Jimmy: Or crossing the river during that storm.

Ezra: That's one folks will write about.

Jimmy: All those prisoners we took in Trenton? I can't wait to tell my father about it. (*Pause.*) When I see him.

Mary pops up.

Mary: Tell me, Jimmy.

Jimmy: Mary, you, you shouldn't be here.

Mary: Why not? (*Sally joins here.*)

Martin: Yes, why not? (*To Sally and then Mary, he tops his hat*) Good morning.

Jimmy: Because we're on our way to battle, that's why.

Martin: You have time to tell them about yesterday in Trenton.

Sally: Aye, do for we heard the guns nearly the entire day.

Jimmy: Well, Ezra can tell you about that.

Ezra: What you ladies heard were the men, me among them, with Colonel Hand. There were six hundred of us. Riflemen all. Our duty was simple. Keep Cornwallis and his men out of Trenton for as long as we could. These Regulars marched along the King's highway (*Points toward Rt. 206.*) Over five thousand men he had with him and all wanting to get to us. We held 'em back by taking shots whenever we could and then disappearin' back into the trees. We kept that up all the way into Trent Town, keeping the Regulars delayed until Washington could get our army over the bridge and up the hill. It was some of the most pleasurable shootin' I've ever done.

Mary: And then what happened?

Jimmy: As Ezra said, we were to cross the Assunpink to take our positions on the hill. There's only the one bridge across to it was crowded crossing it. We could hear the riflemen and Cornwallis' troops firing. Closer and closer they came.

Martin: We knew Hessians marched with them, Hessians out for revenge.

Jimmy: General Washington sat on his horse in the middle of the bridge watching us we crossed. I was pushed over by the force of so many of us. I found myself leaning against the general's horse. But the horse didn't flinch or move or seem bothered at all. I looked up at the general. He was as calm as his horse. He looked me in the eye, and then said, "Move along son, and keep safe." (*Pauses.*) I'll never forget that, Mary.

Mary: No. Never.

Martin: All those Regulars and Hessians think we can't fight, but we showed 'em.

Ezra. We outfoxed them twice and today is the third time.

Sally: What do you mean, sir?

Ezra: We pulled out of Trenton at midnight last night. Silent as mice, we tied rags around the wagon wheels and kept our tongues still. Before we left, we made huge fires that lit up the sky. This we did to fool the

Regulars into thinkin' we were restin' and waitin' for the morning and a full-scale attack.

Martin. They'll be disappointed to see we haven't stayed for their tea party.

Ezra: And they sent us such a lovely invitation.

The five of them laugh.

Mary: And what are you doing here?

Martin: There's a small garrison in Princeton and plenty of stores. We mean to take both.

Suddenly Jimmy is distracted by something he notices in the distance.

Jimmy: (*Looking off into the distance*) What was that?

Martin: What?

Jimmy: Something caught the sunlight, off in the distance.

Ezra: Some farmer tending to his business no doubt.

Martin: I must leave you here as I am attached to General Mercer and we are to destroy the bridge over the Stony Brook.

Jimmy and Ezra return to the woods while Martin runs ahead. Mary and Sally follow Jimmie and Ezra into the woods.

Annis: Martin is in a hurry. Come. Let's follow. *(Follow Martin up the Eastern trail until he disappears back into the woods. Annis stops the group.)* Wait, I hear something. *(She leads them a little further up the trail.)*

Scene 3

From out of the woods come two British Soldiers. They look out across the trail. One points to something. The other sees it also. They step back into the woods. From across the trail, two American Soldiers step out of the woods. They repeat the actions of the British. They return to the woods.

With the Tourists in the center of the trail, the two British soldiers again step out of the wood. From across the trail steps Colonel Mawhood.

Mawhood: Come about! Come about! Quick march!
Annis: Ho! What's this?

Harry: Sir, I see an officer! A general he is!

Brigadier General Hugh Mercer steps out of the woods as the Brits steps back to hide behind trees. Martin steps out of the woods to follow Mercer. He is joined be a second soldier. The Brits raise their guns prepared to fire.

Mercer: Men! Bring up the artillery!

Martin: Sir, where shall we position it?

Mercer: Around that barn. (*He points to the same trees the Brits hide behind.*)

Harry: (*Loud whisper*) Stay put, lads, they're coming.

Mercer and men approach the barn (trees.) The Brits step out and fire on them. Mercer is knocked to the ground. Martin runs into the woods and the second American fires his weapon toward the Brits. Harry runs out to stand over Mercer. Note: keep the Tourists out of the line of fire, but make it loud and smoky.

Harry: Now what have we here?

Mercer shakes his head and then stands up, draws his sword.

Mercer: I'll thow ye what ye have here. (*He attacks the Harry but then the second Brit runs up with bayonet at the read.*)

The American soldier is obviously frightened.

Mercer: Stand fast, men, reinforcements are on the way!

Harry, Mercer, and their men engage in fighting. Mercer is hit on the side of the head by a gun butt. He staggers for a second.

Harry: Ask for quarter, you damn rebel general!

Mercer: Rebel! The devil take you all!

Mercer is hit a second time by a British butt, which brings him to his knees. He lashes out with his sword, the Brits stab him repeatedly. He bleeds profusely. He is left for dead. The American soldier runs into the woods.

Annis: Oh my, we are in the middle of this battle. Come, this way! Quickly now for I see even more soldiers arriving onto the field.

Annis moves the Tourists forward. As they walk, soldiers come in and around the trail, firing shots off. Washington crosses the trail, pauses, a shot is heard, and then he disappears into the trees.

Scene 5

Mary and Sally dash out of the trees. They stop.

Mary: How do we get back home? The soldiers are firing everywhere!

The SOUND OF A CANNON is loud nearby. Both girls scream and crouch to the ground. Across the way dashes

Captain William Shippin, a Continental Marine. He spots the girls and runs to them. Behind him comes Peter.

Shippin: What are you girls doing here?

Mary: We followed the soldiers.

Shippin: You can't stay here. Peter?

Peter: Yes Captain.

Shippin: See that barn yonder?

Peter: Yes sir, I do.

Shippin: (*To Sally*) Whose barn is that?

Sally: Thomas Clarke's, sir.

Shippin: (*To Peter*) Take them over there. Hide them under whatever you can. Then meet us on the battlefield. (*Shippin begins to march on.*)

Sally: Sir! (*Shippin halts, turns back to face Sally*) Who are ye?

Shippin: William Shippin, Captain, Continental Marines at your service. (*He tips his hat to her, turns to leave.*)

Sally: From where?

Shippin: (*Over his shoulder*) Philadelphia.

Shippin disappears into the woods. Peter helps the girls up and they run off in the opposite direction into the woods.

Annis: It is fortunate that those Marines discovered them. I'm certain young Peter will get them to the safety of Thomas Clarke's barn.

SOUND OF CANNON.

Annis: I think it best that we discover some safety!

Annis leads the Tourists on up the trail. But they run into more soldiers that seem to be running away from the battle. Washington steps out, draws his sword and steps in the midst of the soldiers running around.

Washington: Stop! Turn around! Go back into the battle for there are more of us than them. Follow me men, we can win the day!

The soldiers follow Washington off. Annis and the Tourist follow to the next scene. On the way, soldiers come in and out of the woods and fire their weapons.

Scene 6

From out of the trees comes Captain Shippin. He staggers forward, clutching his stomach. He then falls to his to his knees. A moment later, Peter follows.

Peter: Captain? Captain, there you are.

Shippin: Peter? Is it over?

Peter: Washington is pursuing the Regulars.

Shippin: He is alive?

Peter: Yes, he is.

Shippin: I was stunned after I was hit. Tell me, what happened?

Peter: After Mercer went down the men routed.

Shippin: Mercer is dead?

Peter: Honestly sir, I don't know. Most likely. He was bayoneted, repeatedly.

Shippin: He was a good man. But continue, Peter, what happened then?

Peter: You remember sir, Washington had to convince the men to return to the fight.

Shippin: But not us, Peter, not the Marines.

Peter: No sir, not us. We never left the battle.

Shippin: And then what happened?

Peter: Washington led the way. He galloped his horse out on that field and the men followed. His horse reared up on his legs as Washington spoke. It was a sight. Don't you recall that Captain?

Shippin: Yes, I think I do.

Peter: You could see some of the men were frightened, but when they saw their commander leading the charge there was no choice but to follow such righteous courage. Because that courage rubbed off on us all. So into the thick of it he road and we right behind him fanning out across the fields of these two farms.

Shippin: Into the battle? Into the flanks, you mean? To urge the men on from the sides?

Peter: No, Captain. I mean into the middle of it.

Shippin: (*Pauses to think*) Yes! I remember it now.

Peter: Because you were there, sir, in the midst yourself.

Shippin: I was in the frontal attack. I had just fired my weapon when I heard a great shout coming from behind me. I stepped to the side, to reload and to try and see what had happened among the men.

Peter: It was him, Washington, racing onto the field.

Shippin: Yes. I was afraid for him, that he would be killed.

Peter: Without turning your back to the enemy, you ran, backwards, then fired your weapon upon some poor fool who lies drenched in his own blood.

Shippin: I knelt down, not too far from him, I reloaded again.

Peter: Washington rode to the center, in between the enemy and us.

Shippin: He is our ideal, of what should be done. I remember standing, thinking to shield him…

Peter. So you did.

Shippin: And I can remember nothing else save an awful roar of fire.

Peter: Both sides fired, at the same time. Guns, cannon, all conspired to bring him, and all men, down. (*Slight pause*) The last thing I saw was you, Captain. You leapt up, as if to catch something. Then a great smoke filled the air, like a thick fog. There was no breeze to vanquish the smoke, so, for what seemed an eternity, we could see nothing. We were petrified, that when the smoke cleared, we should be without our commander.

Shippin: (*Grabbing Peter's arm.*) And?

Peter: The smoke lifted enough so that we could see him, the general, still sitting upon his horse.

Shippin: Wounded?

Peter: No.

Shippin: Not anything?

Peter: Not a scratch.

Shippin: (*Relieved*) I am pleased to hear it.

Peter: We all were pleased. (*Turns to face Shippin*) But you, Captain, you, I am afraid, did not fare as well.

Shippin: What does that matter?

Peter: It matters to me. William Shippin, you have been like an older brother to me. You have kept me alive.

Shippin: We have kept each other afloat during these past few months.

Peter: I have not been much help to you in this battle at Princeton.

Shippin: You are here with me now. Your arm, Peter, it does not look to be of much use to you.

Peter: (Feeling for arm) Cannon.

Shippin: Does it cause you much pain?

Peter: I feel nothing.

Shippin: Neither do I. (*Looks at wound*) It's clean through my gut, Peter.

Peter: Yes, I know.

Shippin: Why don't I feel it?

Peter: You don't know?

Shippin: Know what?

Peter: Captain, when they fired upon our general, you jumped up to shield his body.

Shippin: I begin to have a sense of what has really happened to me.

Peter: Do you sir?

Shippin: Peter, am I…

Peter: Yes, you are dead, sir.

Shippin: And you?

Peter: Dead as dead can be.

Shippin: Well, this is a fine state of affairs. How are we to fight for our country this way?

Peter: I'm not certain. Though I think I have an idea.

Shippin: What's that?

Peter: We can be ghosts of this battlefield, and haunt anyone who doesn't give it respect. We can inspire others to keep the Cause going. And, every once in awhile, like right now, we can do a little lingering to remind folks so that they don't forget us.

Shippin: You mean like these folks here in front of us?

Peter: What folks?

Shippin: Right there. (*To the Tourists*) Don't forget us. All right? Read your history, and come out to this battlefield to take care of it as well as to have a fun. (*To Peter*) Come on now, Peter, let's rejoin our Marine troops on their way to Nassau Hall.

Peter: (*to group*) If you would like to pay your respects to the soldiers who died here, like the captain and myself, I am buried up over across the way, by those columns up on the hill. Come by any time, but don't fret, I won't haunt you. (*As he walks to the woods with Shippin*) I only come out on times this. Do come back and see us again, next year.

Peter and Shippin disappear into the woods.

Annis: Such brave men. Do you know where the columns are? Right up that hill, where those British soldiers spotted the Americans for the first time. There are many fine soldiers buried there, British and American.

Scene 7 (on the trail)

Several Continentals come running up the trail along with Jimmy beating loudly on his drum.

A Continental: Come men, the field is ours! On now to Nassau Hall!

The Continentals give a shout and follow, at a run, after the first one.

Annis: (*To the Tourists*) Out of the way, out of the way!

The soldiers then disappear into the woods except for Jimmy, who segues his battle beat into a slow and mournful one. He stays with the tourists until they approach the next scene.

Scene 8

January 12, 1777. Back bedroom, the Clarke House. The severely wounded General Mercer lies in bed. Hannah Clarke attends to him. Thomas Clarke, her brother, enters.

Mercer: What has happened?

Thomas: Thee won the battle.

Mercer: Washington?

Hannah: Gone on to Morristown, with his army.

Thomas: Thou wast in a daze after thou wast found, wounded yet breathing, leaning against the oak down the hill, near by my brother's barn. Cornwallis was at the bridge point and pressing his men across the brook so Washington needed to make haste.

Mercer: Aside from yourselves, who attends me?

Hannah: Dr. Rush. Poor man, he needs sleep. Day and night he makes his rounds, first here then the Meeting House where more poor souls lay sick, wounded or dying. He attended to my sister-in-law as well.

Mercer: Why is that?

Hannah: She suffered the loss of her child in the womb.

Mercer: A miscarriage? Was this awful battle the cause of it?

Hannah: No. Though who can say with all the stimulation these past weeks... They hid her in the basement as the shooting started. Carried her down, bed and all. The Regulars were not kind to her once the Continentals had left. Most distressing it has been these past few days.

Thomas: Lesser men it was who thought to question her in a rough manner, but then Cornwallis put a stop to it.

Mercer: I am sorry for the trouble it has caused you both for I see you have worked tirelessly to care for *all* men wounded in this battle.

Hannah: It makes little difference to a man, as he lay dying, whether he is Rebel or Regular. I doubt if God recognizes such differences.

Mercer: Aye good mistress Clarke. That must be the way of it where men have no say. All the same, as I lay dying I thank you, and your brother, for your kindness.

Thomas: Surely general, thee will recover.

Hannah: Aye, General Mercer. Your wounds heal.

Mercer: I think not.

Thomas: Thee would have fared better if the British would had given thee the asked for quarter.

Mercer: No, that is not the way of it, and I must tell you how it was before I die.

Hannah: You'll not die this day, General Mercer.

Mercer: I will die soon.

Hannah: (*pointing out wounds on chest*) These wounds seem to heal.

Mercer: This is what shall kill me. (*He raises his arm*)

Hannah: (*Gasps*) but Dr. Rush-

Mercer: ...has done what he can. Attend my words. (*The Clarkes and Sally gather near.*) When I received the second blow to the head, the Regulars bade me give up. They called me Rebel. Me. Hugh Mercer. They cannot know how I think of *them* as rebels, who overthrew the rightful king of England, for that German.

Hannah: You speak of the troubles of 1746, and of Bonny Prince Charlie.

Mercer: I do. At Culloden.

Thomas: A terrible day for the Scots who sided with Charles Stewart. Which thee did?

Mercer: Yes. After the battle they hunted us down as if we were rabid dogs, killing or taking us prisoners to be sold into slavery. I hid myself in out of the way places for a year before I had money enough to come to America. But once here, all that terror was forgotten.

Hannah: Until the Third of January?

Mercer: Aye, Mistress Clarke, until then, (*becoming agitated*) when they spoke to me as they did and I in my own land, not theirs!

Hannah: You must lie still, General Mercer.

Mercer: I don't mean to be trouble…

Hannah: You're none at all, if you stay quiet and don't rile yourself so. The battle is over, you have won, and for myself, I am relieved. Tis not anything I would ever wish to live through again.

Mercer: I am sorry for it having to be here, on this farm. And you being Friends.

Thomas: Twas William's farm that felt the brunt of it.

Hannah: In William's orchard they fired upon ye first.

Thomas: Thee was telling us of the stabbing thee took.

Mercer: Aye. I will set the record aright. I would not give them the pleasure of my asking for their mercy. I sought no quarter from them and accept my punishment accordingly. That I angered them, and these wounds are their response, tis only what was expected. *(sighs deeply)* What day is it?

Thomas: First Day.

Mercer: How many days since the battle?

Thomas: Nine.

Hannah: Tis the 12th day of January.

Mercer: I feel someone here in the room with me.

Thomas: (*Leans in close to Mercer*) Sometimes the Regulars come into the room.

Mercer: No, someone else. (*Turns his head towards the Tourists*) Them.

Thomas: Them?

Hannah: The guests standing out there. Tell them, Thomas, how they can see the room where this great man died.

Thomas: (*Spoken to the tourists*) In our home, the small bedroom in front. Do you know where that is?

Annis: (*If no response, Annis may chime in*) Do you? (*Wait for responses from Tourists*)

Mercer: Have you seen it, then? The place where I died?

Wait for tourist response. Annis may again urge a response or assist the Tourists in the interaction.

Thomas: They have named the county after you, General. That is more than I can say for the Clarkes.

Hannah: And the new road in back.

Mercer: (*to tourists*) Is that so?

Wait for tourist response.

Thomas: (*To Mercer*) Thee is buried in Philadelphia.

Hannah: And you have two famous descendents.

Mercer: I do?

Thomas: General George S. Patton, and a songwriter, Johnny Mercer.

Mercer: A general and a writer of songs. Tis no mean feat for a penniless refugee from Scotland. (*Turns to the tourists*) You will not forget us, now that you have met us? You will come back to this place, for a visit?

Annis: I think they will. Will you come back?

Thomas: And please, all of *you*; don't forget that we are no longer here to take care of the house, so will you do that for us? (*Slight pause, and then pointedly.*) Will you take care of our house?

Wait for tourist response.

Hannah: Thank you for your visit. Come back again, soon.

Annis: Thank you.

As the scene fades, Annis begins to move the Tourists to the ending area.

Annis: I must leave you now and return to my home. There I will write poems about this day and General Washington. Please enter the Clarke House and see all that it has to offer.

The End

Contacts

The author
lauraspeaks@mac.com

Princeton Battlefield Society
Jerry Hurwitz, President
redcoat43d@aol.com

Princeton Battlefield State Park
John Mills, Site historical specialist
pbsp@aol.com

Princeton Battlefield State Park
500 Mercer Road
Princeton, NJ

Park is open from dawn to dusk. Clarke House
Museum is open Wednesday through Sunday. Call
ahead for hours as they change due to cut backs in
New Jersey (like every other state!) 609.921.0072

Now available....

www.ingramcontent.com/pod-product-compliance
Lightning Source LLC
Chambersburg PA
CBHW021911040426
42447CB00007B/804